This Keepsake
Journal Belongs To

_____

"I will remember the works of the LORD: surely I will remember thy wonders of old"

Psalm 77:11

Remembering

God's Faithfulness

A Keepsake Journal to Reflect on and
Record What God Has Done
in Your Life

LOIS FORCET

ISBN: 979-8-9865990-5-2

Introduction

What events in your life has God demonstrated His faithfulness? How often do you take the time to stop and remember what He has done; how he has kept you and has brought you out on the other side of numerous trials? Psalm 77:11 reminds us to not forget God's goodness but instead, to remember them.

"I will remember the works of the LORD: surely I will remember thy wonders of old" (KJV)

It is a must that you spend daily time in prayer, expressing your praise and gratitude for God's abundant grace and mercies. Maintaining a remembrance journal is another way to keep in the forefront of your mind all the ways in which God has shown how faithful He is today as well as in the past. With this keepsake journal, you'll have the opportunity to reflect on, and write down specific events that have taken place in your life in which God has been faithful to you or has intervened on your behalf. Whether it's an answered prayer or something you know that only He could have done, go ahead and write it down so you'll never forget! What a blessing it will be for you to have a recount of these experiences to revisit when needed. It's so easy to forget, especially during difficult times. The tendency is to focus on the negative, shifting our eyes away from God who has kept and provided for us in so many other circumstances. Remembering His faithfulness strengthens our faith as we keep our minds and hearts focused, instead, on Him!

Date:

Date:

Date:

Date:

Date:

Date:

Date:

Date:

Date:

Date:

Date:

Date:

Date:

Date:

Date:

Date:

Date:

Date:

Date:

Date:

Date:

Date:

Date:

Date:

Date:

Date:

Date:

Date:

Date:

Date:

Date:

Date:

Date:

Date:

Date:

Date:

Date:

Date:

Date:

Date:

Date:

Date:

Date:

Date:

Date:

Date:

Date:

Date:

Date:

Date:

Date:

Date:

Date:

Date:

Date:

Date:

Date:

Date:

Date:

Date:

Date:

Date:

Date:

Date:

Date:

Date:

Date:

Date:

Date:

Date:

Date:

Date:

Date:

Date:

Date:

Date:

Date:

Date:

Date:

Date:

Date:

Date:

Date:

Date:

Date:

Date:

Date:

Date:

Date:

Date:

Date:

Date:

Date:

Date:

Date:

Date:

Date:

Date:

Date:

Date:

Date:

Date:

Date:

Date:

Date:

Date:

Date:

Date:

Date:

Date:

Date:

Date:

Date:

Date:

Date:

Made in United States
Orlando, FL
05 February 2023